j 972.96
McCulla, Patricia E.
Bahamas
Philadelphia, Pa. : Chelsea
House Publishers, 1999.

09   10   ILL09
 1   1   1

⊰BAHAMAS⊱

MAJOR WORLD NATIONS

BAHAMAS

Patricia E. McCulla

CHELSEA HOUSE PUBLISHERS
Philadelphia

Chelsea House Publishers

Contributing Author: Derek Davis

3   5   7   9   8   6   4

Library of Congress Cataloging-in-Publication Data

McCulla, Patricia E.
Bahamas.
Includes index.

Summary: Surveys the history, topography, people,
and culture of the Bahamas, with an emphasis on the
country's current economy, industry, and place in the
political world.

1. Bahamas. [1. Bahamas]
1. Title
F1651.M14   1987   972.96   87-11664

ISBN 0-7910-4755-5

◄ C O N T E N T S ►

GRAND
BAHAMA

THE ABACOS

Freeport

ATLANTIC
OCEAN

BIMINI
ISLANDS

BERRY
ISLANDS

ELEUTHERA

PARADISE
ISLAND

NASSAU

NEW
PROVIDENCE

CAT ISLAND

TONGUE
OF THE
OCEAN

EXUMA
SOUND

SAN
SALVADOR

ANDROS

RUM CAY

EXUMA
ISLANDS

LONG ISLAND

RAGGED
ISLAND
RANGE

B A H A M A S

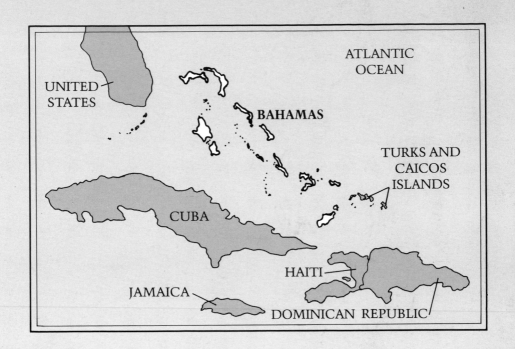

ATLANTIC OCEAN

UNITED STATES

BAHAMAS

TURKS AND CAICOS ISLANDS

CUBA

HAITI

JAMAICA

DOMINICAN REPUBLIC

Tropic of Cancer

CROOKED ISLAND

MAYAGUANA

ACKLINS

LITTLE INAGUA

GREAT INAGUA

N

◄ FACTS AT A GLANCE ►

Land and People

Area	5,382 square miles (13,993 square kilometers)
Total Number of Islands	700
Number of Occupied Islands	40
Highest Point	Mount Alvernia on Cat Island, 206 feet (62 meters)
Population	270,000
Population Density	50 people per square mile (20 per sq km)
Population Distribution	Urban, 84 percent; rural, 16 percent
Most Populous Islands	New Providence and Grand Bahama
Capital	Nassau
Other Major City	Freeport
Official Language	English
Literacy Rate	85 percent
Ethnic Groups	Black, 72 percent; mulatto, 14 percent; white, 13 percent; Asian, 1 percent
Religion	Baptist and Church of God, 42 percent; Roman Catholic, 19 percent; Anglican, 20 percent; other, 19 percent
Average Life Expectancy	Male, 68 years; female, 77 years
Infant Mortality	20/1,000 live births

Economy

Gross Domestic Product	$4 billion
Unemployment Rate	15 percent
Major Industry	Tourism, which accounts for about 60 percent of income, 50 percent of employment, and 3.4 million tourists annually
Other Industries	Banking, finance, oil refining, chemical manufacturing, drug manufacturing, salt production, and rum distilling
Exports	Fruits, vegetables, fish, salt, aragonite, chemicals
Currency	Bahamian dollar, divided into 100 cents; equal in value to U.S. dollar

Government

Form of Government	Parliament with two legislative houses
Formal Head of Government	Queen Elizabeth II, represented by Governor-General
Head of Government	Prime minister
House of Assembly	40 representatives elected by citizens
Senate	16 members appointed by the governor, prime minister, and opposition leader
Judicial System	Three appointed judges preside over the Court of Appeals, the nation's highest court.
International Affiliations	The Commonwealth of Nations, the United Nations, and a variety of Caribbean organizations.

◄HISTORY AT A GLANCE►

about 800 A.D.	The Lucayan Indians arrive in the Bahamas. They set up a farming and fishing culture.
1492	Christopher Columbus lands in the eastern Bahamas during his first voyage to the New World.
1500 to 1520	Spain carries off all 40,000 Lucayan Indians to work in its gold mines, pearl fisheries, and plantations.
1629	King Charles I of England grants the Bahamas to Sir Robert Heath.
1648	The first 70 settlers, the "Eleutherian Adventurers," arrive from Bermuda seeking religious freedom. Others follow. The settlers establish Charles Town on New Providence.
1670	At the request of the settlers, England gives control of the islands to the Lord Proprietors of the Carolinas.
1684	The Spanish attack New Providence and wipe out Charles Town.
1686	New settlers arrive from Jamaica.
1688 to 1693	Pirates abound in the region and Governor Cadwaller Jones encourages them to use the Bahamas as a base.
1694	The Lord Proprietors appoint Nicholas Trott governor. He rebuilds Charles Town and renames it Nassau.

1703	The French and Spanish attack Nassau. Subsequent raids destroy New Providence.
1706	Organized government breaks down and the pirates take control. One pirate leader is Edward Teach, or Blackbeard.
1717	The Lord Proprietors give up control of the islands to the English monarch.
1718	King George I appoints Woodes Rogers governor of the Bahamas. Governor Rogers drives out the pirates and works to rebuild Nassau until his death in 1732.
1741	Fort Montagu is built and Fort Nassau is strengthened.
1775 to 1781	The islands serve as a British supply base during the American Revolution. In 1776 and 1778, the United States attacks Nassau to capture British supplies.
1782	Spanish and United States forces join to capture Nassau.
1783	The Treaty of Versailles restores the Bahamas to England. Many settlers arrive from Florida.
1838	Black slaves are freed in the islands.
1861 to 1865	Blockade runners use the islands to ship supplies to the Confederates during the Civil War.
1866	A severe hurricane and a typhoid epidemic devastate the islands.
1905 to 1919	Sponges become the mainstay of the Bahamian economy.
1938	A fungus attacks the sponges and helps destroy the sponge industry.
1940	Britain appoints the duke of Windsor governor, and the islands begin to become fashionable resorts.

1949 The Bahamian government passes the Hotels Encouragement Act to promote development and tourism.

1953 William Cartwright forms the Progressive Liberal party (PLP), dedicated to working for the good of all Bahamians.

1958 White businessmen form the United Bahamian party (UBP).

1963 England grants the Bahamas internal self-government.

1973 The Commonwealth of the Bahamas becomes an independent nation within the Commonwealth of Nations.

1992 The Free National movement, formed by UBP members and PLP dissidents, wins election and takes control of the government.

Tourist attractions such as El Casino on Freeport evoke the Bahamas's resort image, but the islands have more than beaches and sunshine.

The Bahamas and the World

When most people think of the Bahamas, they imagine an international tourist resort with sunny beaches, beautiful blue water, and luxurious hotels and casinos. In many ways, this picture of the Bahamas is accurate. Millions of visitors travel to the Bahamas every year. About 60 percent of the nation's income comes from tourism. And about 50 percent of all Bahamians work in the tourist industry.

The Bahamas is much more than a popular resort, however. This chain of islands off the Florida coast also has a reputation as an international center for banking and finance. Its tax and banking regulations have attracted hundreds of banks and investment management companies. Other industries have given the Bahamas several important trading partners. Oil refining, chemical manufacturing, and other industries provide exports for trade with the United States, the United Kingdom, and Canada. For its imports, such as crude oil, food, and manufactured goods, the Bahamas trades with the United States, Saudi Arabia, Nigeria, and Libya.

But the Bahamas's international significance does not end there. The Commonwealth of the Bahamas, as it is officially known, is a member of the Commonwealth of Nations, the United Nations, and numerous other international organizations.

Oil refining and other heavy industries have diversified the Bahamas's economy.

In the past, the world has seen the Bahamas in many other ways. When Christopher Columbus discovered the islands in 1492, he used the Spanish word *bajamar*, or "low water," to describe the shallow sea around the islands, thus christening the Bahamas. In this new world, he saw no gold or great cities. Instead he found primitive Indians, whom the Spanish soon took away to work as slaves in other colonies.

In the 1600s, English colonists saw the Bahamas as a haven for religious freedom. At the same time, pirates saw the islands as a perfect base for operations. Conflicts between the colonists and the pirates took many years to settle. During the American Revolution, the Bahamas islands served as a supply base for the British, and throughout the Civil War, they sheltered blockade runners. Because of the Bahamas's history of piracy and smuggling, many people naturally thought of the islands as a headquarters for rum-running during the Prohibition era in the United States.

In the 1940s, the world began to see the Bahamas as a fashionable resort. The duke of Windsor's appointment as governor and the passage of laws to encourage tourism helped promote this image. Since then, the Bahamas's reputation has grown and the nation has prospered and become independent.

Today the Bahamas presents at least three distinct faces to the world—faces that reflect its diverse islands and their cultures. Nassau, the capital, located on New Providence Island, combines colonial charm with its status as an international resort and financial center. Freeport, on Grand Bahama Island, is a glamorous, modern city with a cosmopolitan flavor. Small villages on the other islands have changed little in the past several hundred years.

More than 270,000 whites, blacks, and mulattoes (people of mixed race) live on these islands. Most are descendants of the black slaves and white settlers who colonized the area. The Bahamians inhabit only 40 of the 700 islands that comprise the Bahamas. And more than three-quarters of the population lives on the most developed islands: New Providence and Grand Bahama. The rest of the Bahamians live on the Family Islands, the name they use for the other islands in the chain. But no matter where they live Bahamians are proud of their land and their history, and they look forward to a prosperous future.

Rose Island's rugged coast typifies the Bahamas's topography. Scientists believe that the islands are the flattened peaks of a mountain chain.

The Isles of June

In the Atlantic Ocean, off the southeastern coast of Florida, lies a large group of islands whose climate George Washington once described as "perpetual June." These "Isles of June," as the Bahamas are sometimes known, are actually an archipelago, or island chain.

The archipelago includes an estimated 700 islands and 2,300 rocks and cays (pronounced "keys"), or low-lying islands. Straddling the Tropic of Cancer, the islands stretch from about 50 miles (80 kilometers) east of Florida to about 50 miles (80 km) north of Haiti. They extend 200 miles (320 km) from east to west and 550 miles (880 km) from north to south. Although this area totals more than 100,000 square miles (260,000 square kilometers), only 5,382 square miles (13,993 sq km) of this territory is land.

Geologists believe that the Bahama islands are the flattened peaks of a great underwater mountain range. The deep channels between the islands are vast valleys that drop as low as 10,000 feet (3,030 meters) to the ocean floor. The terrain of the Bahamas includes seaside cliffs, dense jungles, and isolated beaches and coves. On most of the islands, the highest point is only about 100 feet (30 m) above sea level. The highest point overall is Mount Alvernia on Cat Island, which rises only 206 feet (62 m) above sea level.

The archipelago is made of limestone—the only type of rock found in the Bahamas. It formed over millions of years as layers of limestone built up. In many places, the limestone foundation is several thousand feet thick.

The Bahamas is very barren. On most of the islands, the land is rocky or covered with a thin layer of soil. Natural vegetation consists mostly of pine forests and evergreens, although cactus grows on the drier islands. The existing soil is fertile, but it is often lodged in rock crevices and holes that form when water dissolves the limestone surface. In some places, deep caves and potholes scar the land,

The islands' coral reefs provide a lush habitat for underwater plants and marine life.

making it impossible to farm efficiently. Farmers must use dynamite to enlarge pockets of tillable earth. In others, they must use machinery to break up the overlying rock layer and expose the softer, underlying land for pasture or farming.

The Bahamas has no permanent rivers or streams because rainwater sinks into the limestone. Most of the fresh water on the islands is found close to the surfaces of lakes and wells, resting on top of the salt water. If Bahamians drill their wells too deeply or work them too hard, the water becomes brackish as the salt water surfaces. The depth of freshwater wells depends on the amount of rainwater that sinks into the ground. More fresh water is found on the wetter, northwest islands of Abaco, Andros, and Grand Bahama than on the drier, southeast islands of Acklins, Mayaguana, and Inagua.

Sometimes fresh water is found in "boiling holes." These appear when tides allow fresh water to flow through connecting passages between the land and the sea. Sometimes ocean water surfaces inland, as in the Ocean Hole on Eleuthera, in which visitors can view marine life. Divers enjoy ocean "blue holes," found off the shores of several islands. These holes are actually columns of fresh water that rise from buried caves in the ocean bed.

The Coral Reefs

The water surrounding the Bahamas is filled with coral reefs—ridges of layered limestone that form when tiny sea creatures called polyps shed their brilliantly colored skeletons. Coral reefs serve two important functions. They form the basis of marine life in the area, providing homes and feeding grounds for many fish. They also protect the low-lying islands from erosion by the ocean. The warm, shallow waters of the islands help the coral reefs develop. Most coral reefs lie on the windward, or northern, shores of the islands, where strong winds constantly supply the polyps with fresh food blown toward shore.

These favorable conditions allow three types of coral reefs to form in the Bahamas: fringe reefs, barrier reefs, and atolls. Fringe reefs are tall structures that exist at the edge of the shallow water around almost every island. Barrier reefs, separated from the mainland by a wide lagoon, protect the eastern shore of Andros and the bight (bend in the coast) in Acklins. Atolls develop when coral surrounds a land mass that later sinks, forming a circular lagoon.

The Climate

Temperatures in the Bahamas range from subtropical to tropical. In the winter months, the Gulf Stream keeps the islands warm and balmy. On centrally located New Providence, winter temperatures rarely fall below 60° Fahrenheit (15.6° Centigrade) and usually rise to 78° F (25.6° C) in the afternoon. The temperatures are slightly lower in the northern islands and about 5° F (3° C) higher in the southern islands. Summer temperatures tend to be similar throughout the islands, with a low of about 78° F (25.6° C) at night and a high of about 90° F (32.2° C) in the afternoon. Although the weather is humid, tropical breezes lessen the effects of the humidity. They blow predominantly from the east and average less than 10 knots, or 11.51 miles (18.42 kilometers) per hour.

Visitors to the Bahamas find the water temperature as ideal as the coral does. It averages 74° Fahrenheit (23.3° Centigrade) in February and 83° F (28.3° C) in August. The water's salinity, or salt content, is high, so swimmers and snorkelers find it easy to float in the water.

The rainy season usually extends from May through October. The rainfall in Nassau on New Providence averages 46 inches (116 centimeters) a year. The northern islands receive 20 percent more rainfall than Nassau, and the southern islands receive 50 percent less. Rain usually comes in heavy showers or thunderstorms that clear quickly.

The Bahamas's reefs and warm waters attract scuba divers from around the world.

Hurricanes and tropical storms usually hit Nassau between June and November, and most of them occur in August, September, and October. According to records compiled during the last 90 years, Nassau can expect to experience a hurricane once every 9 years.

A Look at the Islands

Centrally located in the Bahamas, New Providence is 21 miles (33.6 kilometers) long and 7 miles (11.2 km) wide, with an area of 58 square miles (150.8 square kilometers). An arched toll bridge joins New Providence to Paradise Island, a long, narrow, 750-acre (300-hectare) sandbar. Although New Providence is one of the smallest islands, more than 175,000 Bahamians—the majority of the people—live there. Most of them live in Nassau, the capital of the Bahamas. The Nassau International Airport is located on the west side of Lake Killarney, a large lake in the center of the island.

Situated at the northwestern end of the Bahamas, Grand Bahama Island is 73 miles (116.8 kilometers) long and 4 to 8 miles (6.4 to 12.8 km) wide, making it the fourth largest island. About 35,000 Bahamians live there, most of them in Freeport, the second largest city in the Bahamas. West End, a resort town on the west side of the island, is only about 50 miles (80 km) from West Palm Beach, Florida.

East of Grand Bahama Island lies the Abacos, a cluster of islands and cays. The Abacos is about 130 miles (208 kilometers) long and has an area of 650 square miles (1,690 square kilometers) of land. A thick growth of tropical pines, especially feathery-needled casuarinas, covers the islands, and wild boar roam the forests. Marsh Harbour, located near the middle of the cluster, is the chief town.

Like many avid fishermen, author Ernest Hemingway set his course for the Biminis.

Serious anglers, or fishermen, often head for the Biminis, two islands south of Grand Bahama. These islands sponsor fishing tournaments from March through August. In the 1930s, American novelist Ernest Hemingway spent a great deal of time fishing in the Biminis. East of the Biminis, the Berry Islands also offer water sports. Many of the islands in this small chain are privately owned.

Andros is the largest and the least explored of the Bahama islands. More than 150 miles (240 kilometers) long and about 45 miles (72 km) across, it lies about 50 miles (80 km) west of New Providence. Its interior is a deep wilderness of pine, mahogany, and bush that shelters ducks, quail, pigeons, partridges, turkey buzzards, doves, pelicans, and parrots. Several channels cut through Andros, dividing it into three islands and many cays. Extensive marshes and mud flats make the west coast uninhabitable. Off its eastern shore, Andros has one of the world's largest barrier reefs. This Bahamian reef drops into a deep channel called the Tongue of the Ocean.

Eleuthera lies east of Andros and New Providence. It measures 110 miles (176 kilometers) long and 5 miles (8 km) across at its widest point and covers about 200 square miles (520 square kilometers). The first white settlers landed here from Bermuda in 1648. A tunnel called Preacher's Cave served as their church and home.

Southeast of Eleuthera is Cat Island, about 150 square miles (390 square kilometers) in size. Like many of the islands, it is long and thin—about 50 miles (80 kilometers) long and from 1 to 4 miles (1.6 to 6.4 km) wide. It has the highest peak in the Bahamas— Mount Alvernia, called Como Hill by residents. At the top of Mount Alvernia is "The Hermitage," a small monastery hand-built by the hermit Father Jerome. Arthur's Town, the primary settlement on the island, is the boyhood home of actor-director Sidney Poitier.

San Salvador, the island believed to be the site of Columbus's first landing in the New World, is located east of Cat Island. San Salvador is a small island, only 14 miles (22.4 kilometers) long and

6 miles (9.6 km) wide. For many years, people called it Watling's Island, after John Watling, a 17th-century pirate who owned a grand home that now lies in ruins at the south end of the island. In 1926, the legislature officially changed the name to San Salvador. Most of the island's 1,000 residents live in the main settlement, Cockburn (pronounced "Coburn") Town.

The waters of Exuma Sound separate Eleuthera from the Exumas, a chain of 365 tiny islands and cays running down the middle of the Bahamas. Although they contain many quiet coves and inlets, many of the islands are uninhabited. The two largest islands are Great Exuma and Little Exuma, where British Loyalists once owned cotton plantations. George Town, the Exumas' largest community, is located on Great Exuma.

Southeast of the Exumas lies a long, narrow island called Long Island. Its hills are almost as high as those on Cat Island and offer views of the Atlantic Ocean and the Caribbean Sea. The island is

Salt mounds abound on Great Inagua, where companies extract sea salt from the ocean.

riddled with caves, and its waters are filled with blue holes. In Deadman's Cay, Indian drawings mark the walls of caves that have never been completely explored. The oldest Spanish church in the Bahamas stands on this island. Stella Maris in the north and Clarence Town in the south are the main settlements.

South of Long Island, Acklins and Crooked Island make up about a 200-square-mile (520-square-kilometer) area near the end of the Bahamas chain. The narrow Crooked Island Passage separates the two islands. Acklins, which covers about 120 square miles (312 sq km), is hilly and serene. Crooked Island, which covers 70 square miles (182 sq km), is marked by deep creeks, caves, and tidal flats, where fishermen have caught record-sized tarpon and bonefish. Its many native herbs are responsible for its reputation as the "Fragrant Island." Colonel Hill on Crooked Island and South West Point on Acklins are the main settlements.

Mayaguana, located east of Acklins Island, covers about 110 square miles (286 square kilometers). Hardwood forests cover most of the island, which remains fairly undeveloped and undisturbed. About 400 people live in Abrahams Bay, Pirates Well, and Betsy Bay on Mayaguana.

Inagua, sometimes called Great Inagua, is the third largest and the southernmost island. On this island, the shallow, marshy waters of Lake Windsor, which is 12 miles (19.2 kilometers) long, attract the largest colony of flamingos in the world (up to 50,000). Inagua Park shelters more than 200 species of birds, including roseate spoonbills, egrets, and hummingbirds. Mounds of salt also feature prominently in the landscape. In fact, the Morton Salt Company extracts sea salt and dries it on Inagua. Matthew Town is the only developed area on the island.

Columbus landed on the Bahamas during his first voyage to the New World and immediately claimed the islands for Spain.

Early History

The first known inhabitants of the Bahamas were the Lucayan Indians, who arrived on the islands in about 800 A.D. A peaceful people, they fished and farmed in a manner still practiced today on parts of the Family Islands. Their culture and language resembled that of the Taino Indians, the natives of Haiti.

Europe learned of the area when Christopher Columbus landed in the eastern Bahamas on October 12, 1492, during his first voyage to the New World. Columbus then sailed from island to island, searching unsuccessfully for gold and great cities. Although the Spanish colonized much of the Caribbean after Columbus's voyage, they never settled in the Bahamas. The infertile soil and lack of gold made the land unappealing. However, the islands did have one resource the Spanish desired: the Lucayans.

The Spanish needed the Lucayans to work in their Caribbean gold mines and plantations and to dive in their pearl fisheries. Between 1500 and 1520, the Spanish carried off the entire Bahamian population—about 40,000 Lucayans. After the Spanish had removed the natives, Spanish ships avoided the Bahamas because of the dangerous rocks and shoals in the area. This left the islands uninhabited for the next 100 years.

In 1629, King Charles I of England gave Sir Robert Heath the Bahamas and a parcel of land in North America that would later be known as the Carolinas. However, the first English settlers did not arrive until 1648, when they fled from Bermuda to seek religious freedom. These first "Eleutherian Adventurers," as they were known, survived a shipwreck off the island they named Eleuthera, after the Greek word for freedom. In their new homeland, they barely eked out an existence as farmers. Other settlers came from Bermuda and many of them landed on the island they dubbed New Providence. In a sheltered location on this island's natural harbor, they established a settlement called Charles Town. It soon became the favorite destination of immigrants to the islands.

In 1670, at the settlers' request, England gave control of the Bahamas to the Lord Proprietors of the Carolinas, who appointed a proprietary governor. However, the new government did not improve the quality of life in the Bahamas. Settlers continued to carve out a

During the 1600s, settlers supported themselves by scavenging goods from wrecked ships.

meager existence by salvaging goods from wrecked ships and by exporting brazilwood and ambergris (an ingredient used to make perfume).

Often, the salvaging of goods from wrecks crossed the line between business and piracy. In 1683, one dispute over a wreck caused English settlers in New Providence to raid Spanish settlements in Florida. Then, in retaliation, the Spanish attacked New Providence and wiped out Charles Town.

A group of immigrants from Jamaica resettled New Providence in 1686. Their leader, Thomas Bridges, became governor in 1688. He was succeeded by Cadwaller Jones, who ruled the Bahamas as a dictator and encouraged pirates to use the island as a base. The Bahamians eventually seized Governor Jones and charged him with high treason. Later, the Lord Proprietors officially fired Jones and, in 1694, appointed Nicholas Trott as his successor.

Trott rebuilt Charles Town and renamed it Nassau, after one of the titles of William III, the English king. He also constructed Fort Nassau, in case the increasing tensions between England and France led to an attack on the islands by France. By 1700, Nassau had 160 houses and 1 church.

But this new prosperity did not last. War finally broke out between England and France in 1702. One year later, France and Spain combined forces to attack Nassau to prevent the English from using the Bahamas as a base for operations. Subsequent raids virtually destroyed New Providence. By 1706, all semblance of organized government had broken down, and pirates had taken undisputed control of the Bahamas. Among the pirate leaders was Edward Teach, also known as Blackbeard.

Because of the governor's incompetence and constant complaints from the few remaining settlers, the Lord Proprietors surrendered the government of the Bahamas to the English crown in 1717. King George I appointed Woodes Rogers governor of the Ba-

In 1718, the British king commissioned Rogers (seated at right) to govern the islands.

hamas in 1718. Rogers took control of the islands from the pirates, reformed the government, and set about rebuilding Nassau and its fort.

Rogers spent his own money on these efforts, and on a trip to London to obtain more funds, he was thrown in a debtors' prison. But the crown reinstated him for a second term, and he returned to the Bahamas in 1729. As his first official act, he called for an elected assembly of 24 members. Rogers continued to improve the government and earn the respect of Bahamians until his death in 1732.

Although Rogers had rid the Bahamas of the threat of pirates, Spain remained an adversary and privateering continued. In 1741, during the War of the Austrian Succession, Nassau was warned of a possible Spanish attack. To bolster Bahamian defenses, Peter Henry Bruce, the governor's second-in-command, refitted Fort Nassau and built Fort Montagu. Throughout this war, the Bahamas served as a privateering base for the English.

The Bahamas also served as a British base during the American Revolution (1775 to 1783). Ships from the newly established United States attacked Nassau in 1776 and again in 1778, to capture British supplies. American forces also helped their allies, the Spanish, attack and capture Nassau in 1782. However, Colonel Andrew Deveaux, a colonist who supported England during the revolution, recruited other British Loyalists and tricked the Spanish into surrendering. The Bahamas was officially restored to the British in 1783 at the signing of the peace treaty at Versailles.

The same treaty gave Florida to Spain. Because many of the Loyalists had fled to Florida during the war, the British government moved these loyal subjects to the Bahamas and gave them land grants to start new lives.

Many of these immigrants had been southern plantation owners with slaves. In their new homeland, they attempted to duplicate the cotton-based economy of the southern states by developing cotton plantations. They also built new churches, schools, and private homes. They even published the first Bahamian newspaper, the *Bahama Gazette*, in August 1784. The Bahamas began to prosper, but its prosperity was short-lived. In 1789, the chenille bug blighted the cotton crop. Insect pests and soil exhaustion soon took their toll.

During a period of prosperity in the late 1700s, Nassau bustled with activity.

Until it was abolished in 1834, slavery kept the Bahamas's cotton plantations profitable.

Problems in the cotton industry forced some white planters to leave the islands. Even greater numbers left in the early 1800s, when the British empire took steps to abolish first the slave trade, and then slavery itself. In 1829, the British appointed Sir James Carmichael Smyth as governor of the Bahamas. He was an abolitionist, a person dedicated to ending slavery. In 1833, the government passed the Abolition of Slavery Act and on August 1, 1834, all slaves were emancipated. After serving four years as paid apprentices to their former masters, they became legally free in 1838.

Economic Troubles

The Bahamas still needed to find an industry that would keep the economy stable. The islands suffered another economic blow when they lost income from salt production on Grand Turk Island in 1848. This occurred when England granted Jamaica jurisdiction over the Turks and Caicos Islands. To compensate for the loss, the government set up the Henega Salt Pond Company in 1849 to develop Inagua's salt ponds. At the same time, however, salt production increased elsewhere in North America, and the United States placed a tariff (tax) on salt, weakening its market.

The Bahamas enjoyed a period of prosperity during the U.S. Civil War (1861 to 1865). Many people found that Nassau was an ideal port for shipping supplies to the Confederates because it was only two or three days away from the blockaded ports of Charleston, South Carolina, and Wilmington, North Carolina. Blockade-running soon became a profitable business. During this period, new buildings sprang up, Nassau's Bay Street was widened, and the Bahamas Police Force was created. Land values appreciated by 300 to 400 percent. Wealthy, boisterous blockade runners filled the new Royal Victoria Hotel, erasing the public debt incurred to build it.

But after the war, poverty again struck the Bahamas. In 1866, typhoid killed many people, and a hurricane devastated the entire archipelago. Rebuilding and repairs drained Nassau's resources, both public and private. Bahamian sailors reverted to scavenging wrecked ships. But the number of shipwrecks off Bahamian shores dwindled

During the U.S. Civil War, the plush Royal Victoria Hotel enjoyed success.

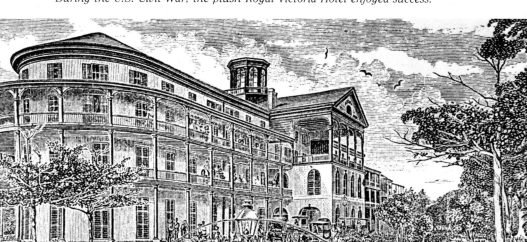

when the government built lighthouses and produced the first accurate charts of the Bahamian waters.

At the close of the 19th century, Bahamians tried to develop various products to help save their economy. They exported conch (pronounced "konk") shells to Europe for use in cameos, but these soon went out of fashion. They tried to grow pineapples and fibrous sisal (a plant used for weaving and rope-making), but the soil soon gave out. Next, the Bahamians turned to the sea and found sponges in their shallow banks. By 1905, one-third of the Bahamians made their living by "sponging." This industry peaked in 1919, when the Bahamas supplied one-quarter of the world's sponges. But by 1938, hurricanes, overfishing, and a sponge fungus had killed the industry.

In an attempt to stabilize their erratic economy, the Bahamians tried to grow sisal, a tropical plant whose fibers can be used to weave rope.

The Bahamian sponge industry was successful until sponge fungus and overfishing destroyed it.

The First World War broke out in 1914. In mid-1915, the British War Office formed a British West Indies Regiment, which many Bahamians joined. The war hurt the islands' economy by limiting imports and exports of food and other products. And when the Bahamian soldiers returned from the war, unemployment rose and economic disaster loomed.

The Bahamas recovered from these problems by returning to illegal seafaring activities. In December 1919, the United States Congress passed the Eighteenth Amendment, known as Prohibition because it prohibited the sale of alcohol. When this happened, rum-running or bootlegging—the smuggling of illegal liquor—became a major industry in the Bahamas. Because they lived only 50 miles (80 kilometers) from the American coast, many Bahamians found it easy to make smuggling runs. This new industry also boosted the

This load of illegal liquor was stopped before it reached the U.S.

Bahamian Treasury because the government taxed the liquor that was imported and later smuggled out.

During the 1920s, the Bahamas also enjoyed a boom in land investment. Pan American Airways instituted a daily flight from Miami to Nassau, and rich Americans began to buy land and build homes on the islands. The land investment boom came to a halt in 1929, when the U.S. stock market crashed, plunging the world into economic depression. However, bootlegging continued to provide the Bahamas with a steady flow of money until Congress repealed Prohibition in 1934.

In the years between the repeal of Prohibition and World War II, the Bahamas suffered another severe economic depression. Some relief came from Harold Oakes, a Canadian millionaire who transferred his enormous wealth to the Bahamas. Oakes bought several thousand acres (hectares) of land and started construction on many projects, such as airports and golf courses, to promote tourism. He employed many local laborers who had been on the brink of starvation. Oakes was elected to the House of Assembly, served in the Legislative Council, and became known as a great benefactor. (Because he was so well liked, Oakes's brutal murder in 1943 shocked the world. Although many Bahamian and foreign detectives worked on the case, his murder remains a mystery.)

Canadian millionaire Oakes spent lavishly to promote the Bahamian tourist industry.

In 1939, the start of World War II in Europe also affected the Bahamas. To get the former English king (the duke of Windsor) out of war-torn Europe, Britain appointed him governor of the Bahamas in 1940. He and the duchess of Windsor, the former Mrs. Simpson (for whom he gave up the crown), attracted wealthy refugees from Europe, and the Bahamas became a fashionable place for the jet set to visit.

The duke (center) and duchess of Windsor attracted fashionable Europeans to the Bahamas.

In 1942, the United States built two naval air bases on New Providence, bringing jobs to many Bahamians. Between 1943 and 1945, New Providence served as a training school for Britain's Royal Air Force, as a staging post on the transatlantic ferry service, and as an ocean patrol and air-sea rescue base during the antisubmarine campaign in the Caribbean and the West Atlantic. These activities brought servicemen to the Bahamas, filling the hotels and helping the economy.

The post-war period brought many economic and political changes to the Bahamas. To support the development of the tourist industry, the government passed the Hotels Encouragement Act of 1949 and appointed Sir Stafford Sands to promote the islands. The development of air conditioning made visiting in the hot summers more comfortable, and the islands began to attract tourists year-round. The government also reinforced its tax-free status to attract foreign investors. These economic advances paved the way for political change.

Black lawyer Lynden O. Pindling joined the PLP and led the "Quiet Revolution" that granted political and economic rights to all Bahamians.

The Quiet
Revolution

By the 1950s, 80 percent of all Bahamians were black. Although they formed the majority of the population, most of them lived like second-class citizens. And when they saw the growing prosperity of the 1950s, they decided they had a right to enjoy it, too. Influenced by the civil rights movement in the United States, a few successful blacks started the "Quiet Revolution," with the motto, "The ballot, not the bullet."

To achieve political changes, William Cartwright, a mulatto magazine publisher, real estate broker, and member of the House of Assembly, formed the Progressive Liberal party (PLP) in 1953. One of the PLP's first recruits was a young, black, Bahamian lawyer who had just finished his training in London. This man, Lynden O. Pindling, would lead his countrymen to equality and independence.

The PLP worked hard to make its presence and position known. Its platform stated that people of all classes, creeds, and religions must work together for the common good. It called for the establishment of voting rights for women and for those who did not own property, a reduction from a seven-year term to a five-year term in the assembly, and the introduction of municipal government. The PLP endorsed equal political representation and other civil rights, as well as better education, agricultural development, lower prices, and strong immigration controls. In the 1956 elections, its efforts began to pay off when PLP candidates won 6 of the 29 seats in the House of Assembly.

The white majority in the assembly—known as the "Bay Street Boys" because many of them owned profitable shops on Nassau's main street—resented the PLP's growing popularity. In 1958, they formed the United Bahamian party (UBP), which black Bahamians nicknamed "Use Black People." Party politics had arrived in the islands.

Bahamians learned the power of a united majority in 1958. When the UBP tried to grant an airport-to-hotel monopoly to tour buses owned by the Bay Street Boys, taxi drivers went on strike and blocked traffic to the airport. Hotel and construction workers joined the strike, and Nassau was at a standstill for 19 days. Through these efforts, the taxi drivers won back the right to transport passengers from the airport to the hotels.

The movement to win wider voting rights gained momentum in the late 1950s. A college student, Doris Johnson, led a women's suffrage movement, even though the UBP government revoked her scholarship. In 1961, after Britain pressured the UBP, the govern-

Dr. Johnson led the women's suffrage movement and later became a Bahamian senator.

ment finally gave women and those who did not own property the right to vote. However, unfair division of voting districts and fear of UBP reprisals kept the PLP from gaining many seats in the 1962 elections.

Despite their differences, both parties saw a need for strengthening the Bahamian government and changing the constitution. In 1963, a constitutional conference gave the Bahamians internal self-government—the first step toward independence. The main constitutional changes included reorganizing the public boards into ministries, changing the Legislative Council into the Senate, and setting up a cabinet and Supreme Court.

The new cabinet was to consist of a premier and at least eight ministers. The governor would appoint the premier, who would act as leader of the Bahamian government. The governor would then appoint the remaining ministers at the premier's suggestion. The governor would also recognize a leader of the opposition party.

When the next general election was held in 1967, the PLP became the majority party. Actually, the PLP and the UBP won the same number of seats, but two independent candidates agreed to support the PLP. Lynden Pindling headed the new administration and appointed the first woman senator, Dr. Doris Johnson. A general

In 1968, Bahamian and British leaders met in London to discuss the independence issue.

*Lynden Pindling (left)
celebrated with other
PLP members after the
1972 elections.*

election in 1968, called after the death of an assembly member,
firmly established the PLP's power.

Now the new administration had a chance to prove itself. It
improved the quality of education by concentrating on teacher training and new school construction. It strengthened the economy by
encouraging foreign investment, expansion of tourism, industrial
development, harbor improvement, revision of tax and license laws,
and stricter immigration controls. The administration also instituted
several public works projects.

In 1968, the new government continued the move toward independence and called for another constitutional conference. The
resulting constitution forced the governor to consult the premier—
now known as the prime minister—on foreign policy matters. It
increased Senate membership to 16 and changed the country's name
to the Commonwealth of the Bahamas.

The government believed that the Bahamas had to achieve economic stability before seeking total independence from Britain. Opponents of independence transformed the UBP into the Free National movement (FNM). They tried to use the threat of communism and the safety of British protection to thwart the move toward independence. Pindling let the people choose in the 1972 elections. A vote for the PLP meant a vote for independence. The people voted for independence, and on July 10, 1973, the Commonwealth of the Bahamas became a free nation within the Commonwealth of Nations.

At that time, a new constitution took effect. It guaranteed the rights for which the PLP had fought. It allowed the governor to remain the official head of state and to represent the queen, but limited his actions to those advised by the government's ministers.

A statue of Columbus stands outside Government House in Nassau. Almost 500 years after Columbus arrived, the Bahamas became a self-governing nation.

Government and Education

The Bahamas has a long history of democratic government. Throughout the last three centuries, the Bahamians have added new rights and freedoms to their constitution. And in turn, each change in the constitution has given them better representation in their government.

Representative government began in the Bahamas in 1671. At that time, royal instructions required the new proprietors to govern with the advice and consent of the islands' freemen, who formed a House of Assembly. In addition to the House of Assembly, the government included a governor, who was appointed by the crown, and the governor's council.

The governor administered the government, controlled its finances, and conducted all judicial business. The governor's council advised him, acted as a court of chancery and appeals, and served as the upper house of the legislature. According to British law, only the British Parliament had the right to legislate for the colonies. However, the Bahamas would recognize a British law only if the Bahamian House of Assembly reenacted it.

For most of the 18th century, the term of service in the assembly was not fixed and tended to be long to avoid the expense of general elections. One parliament lasted nine years. In 1795, the government limited the term to seven years, and in 1962, it reduced the term to five years.

The governor appointed public boards annually. These boards handled public works, education, health, agricultural and marine products, oil exploration, communications, and other areas. Each board had seven members, two of whom had to be members of the House of Assembly.

In theory, the government represented all Bahamians equally. But in reality, it favored the white minority. Although free blacks received the right to vote in 1807, the white minority controlled the government by imposing wealth and property restrictions on voters and candidates for office. Most members of the white minority, who had descended from plantation owners, had moved to New Providence from the Family Islands. But after they moved, many of them continued to represent the Family Islands in the assembly, which led to uneven representation. Their power base remained unchallenged until the 1950s, when the Progressive Liberal party (PLP) gained support.

Modern Bahamian Government

Today the PLP and the Free National movement (FNM), which picked up PLP dissidents and won its first election in 1992, are the dominant parties, forming a sound two-party system. Bahamians participate actively in their government, and most elections draw a 90 percent turnout.

The Bahamian government retains some of the features it developed during its colonial days. It still has a bicameral—or twohouse—legislature, which is made up of the House of Assembly and the Senate. The assembly has 40 elected members and is the stronger house. The Senate has 16 appointed members, at least 4 of whom must be members of the opposition party.

The House of Assembly is part of a bicameral legislature. In 1968, control of the assembly was passed to the PLP in an elaborate ceremony.

The prime minister heads the Bahamian government. He is the majority party leader in the assembly and has a cabinet of at least nine members, who are chosen from the legislature.

The Bahamian judicial system is based on British common law. Magistrate courts serve New Providence and Grand Bahama, and local commissioners administer justice in the Family Islands. The Supreme Court is the next highest court. Its chief justice and other justices are appointed by the governor. They hear civil cases throughout the year, but limit their review of criminal cases to four sessions a year. The highest tribunal is the Court of Appeals. Three judges, appointed by the governor, preside over this court. They are usually

The Bahamas's justice system is centered in this stately courthouse in Nassau.

leading jurists from England or West Indian nations. Their decisions can be appealed to the English Privy Council.

Health Care

British policies have also influenced social services in the Bahamas. For instance, like the British government, the Bahamian government subsidizes medical treatment. Its Ministry of Health owns and operates two hospitals: the Princess Margaret Hospital on New Providence and the Rand Memorial Hospital on Grand Bahama. Charges for treatment are low, and they are waived for patients who cannot pay. A patient can receive care at one of 50 clinics scattered throughout the Family Islands. And if a clinic cannot handle his problem, the patient will be flown to Princess Margaret Hospital. In addition to these socialized hospitals and clinics, the Bahamian health-care system also includes private hospitals and doctors.

The Bahamian government also sponsors a program similar to social security in the United States. Under this program, qualified people can receive retirement, disability, sickness, and maternity benefits, as well as funeral expenses.

Education

The school system in the Bahamas is excellent, and 85 percent of Bahamians can read and write. At the end of each school year, students must take final exams. If they do not pass, they do not move on to the next grade. Bahamian teachers assign several hours of homework every night. In some schools, each student must keep a

At the Princess Margaret Hospital on New Providence, patients who cannot afford to pay for treatment receive free medical care.

homework assignment log. When a student finishes an assignment, his or her parents must sign the logbook to acknowledge that the homework is done.

Bahamian schools follow the British educational system. At age five, children enter the first grade. After following a typical elementary school curriculum through the sixth grade, they enter the "forms." The first three forms are equivalent to junior high school in the United States.

Bahamian students take 8 to 12 subjects during these years, in preparation for the Bahamas General Certificate of Secondary Education Exams. They usually take these exams at age 14 and must pass the five required subjects (English, mathematics, arithmetic, religion, and Bahamian history) before they can leave school or continue on to the next form. Children are only required to attend school between ages 5 and 14 but most continue until at least age 16.

To graduate from the fifth or sixth form (the equivalent of high-school graduation in the United States), students must pass one of two international exams in several different subjects. If a student wants to attend a university, he or she must pass the General Certificate of Education exams. If a student wants to attend a trade school or go to work, he or she must pass the Certificate of Secondary Education exams.

The Bahamas has only one school of higher education, the College of the Bahamas on New Providence. Founded in 1974, this publicly financed, locally oriented college offers many services. Located in Nassau at Oakes Field, it has a teaching division, an extension services division, and a library. It offers a two-year Associate of Arts degree, an Advanced Level General Certificate of Education, a diploma, a certificate, and a Bachelor of Education degree (in association with the University of the West Indies).

The Technical and Vocational Institute, which opened in 1980, teaches basic industrial skills. It offers courses in such fields as electri-

The old Government High School is now the degree-granting College of the Bahamas.

cal installation, plumbing, carpentry, cosmetology, auto mechanics, and painting. Although the center is in New Providence, it also conducts programs on Grand Bahama and some Family Islands.

The Bahamas Hotel Training College, established in 1973, prepares students for jobs in the tourism industry. It trains present and future employees of hotels, tourism organizations, and allied industries. Its apprenticeship program instructs aspiring cooks and waiters. The college also provides on-the-job training for students at its New Providence and Grand Bahama campuses.

The University of the West Indies in Nassau also helps train people for the tourism industry with its Centre for Hotel and Tourism Management. Students in this program participate in internships in the Bahamas or in certain other countries and eventually obtain a Bachelor of Science degree.

The Princess Margaret Hospital maintains a School of Nursing.

Bahamians include blacks of African ancestry, whites of European ancestry, and mulattos (people of mixed race).

The Bahamians and Their Culture

More than 80 percent of the Bahamas's 270,000 residents are black, many of them descendants of the slaves brought to the islands by the British Loyalists. The remaining Bahamians are either white or mulatto (of mixed white and black ancestry). This combination of European and African heritages, along with the constant influence of American tourists, creates a varied cultural environment.

Of the Bahamas's 40 or so inhabited islands, only New Providence and Grand Bahama have genuine cities. The other islands have only small towns and fishing villages. Vast differences exist between life in Nassau and Freeport and life in the other, smaller settlements scattered over the islands.

On the large islands of New Providence and Grand Bahama, residents—both black and white—enjoy a modern, prosperous lifestyle. This was not always the case, however. Although blacks have comprised the majority of the population for centuries, they endured discrimination until the 1950s. Until 1956, they were forbidden to enter theaters, hotels, or restaurants. And until the 1960s, blacks were not welcome in the main shops in Nassau. But thanks to the Quiet Revolution (the Bahamian civil rights movement) and to Prime Minister Pindling's policies—such as limiting the number of work

Many Family Islanders live in simple wooden houses without electricity or plumbing.

permits issued to foreigners and increasing education for black Bahamians—many blacks who live on New Providence and Grand Bahama now belong to a new middle class.

Today, black Bahamians include politicians, bank directors, attorneys, restaurateurs, hotel managers, and entertainers. Middle-class Bahamians of all colors now live much as middle-class Americans do. City-dwelling Bahamian children resemble American children—they wear similar clothes, receive equally good educations, and look forward to the same kinds of employment opportunities.

Bahamians who live on the Family Islands lead very different lives from those in the cities, however. Family Islanders are usually farmers, fishermen, craftspeople, or seasonal resort workers. Many continue to live as their ancestors in the Family Islands did hundreds of years ago and have retained their traditions. The Bahamian government is working to improve roads, electricity, and telecommunications. They are also working to expand and to promote tourism by encouraging ecologically sound hotels.

Children in the Family Islands usually go to school only until age 14, after which schooling is not required. Then they go to work— either in the fields or on fishing boats. Recently, many young Family Islanders have begun to leave their homes to find better opportunities in Nassau. This practice is causing a population imbalance in the Bahamas and an increasing unemployment rate in Nassau.

Although many women in Nassau and Freeport have careers, men remain the breadwinners in the Family Islands. There, women are expected to care for their homes, raise their children, and help in the fields. They may also earn a little money by weaving baskets or creating other handicrafts.

Throughout the islands, the scarcity of tillable farmland has made the sea the Bahamians' main food source. The conch shellfish is one of the nation's favorite foods. Grouper, snapper, and shark are staples, as are crab, crayfish (called "lobster" by the Bahamians), and other shellfish. Beef, lamb, pork, and poultry are widely available. Many Family Islanders also eat exotic meats such as turtle and wild boar.

The sea provides most of the Bahamian diet, including the edible conch shellfish.

Religion and Family Life

The Bahamas's original English settlers brought the Anglican faith with them to the islands. Anglicanism became the first Christian doctrine practiced in the Bahamas, and it remains the state religion. Nevertheless, most Bahamians today practice other faiths. Only 20 percent are Anglican, whereas 50 percent belong to other Protestant religions and 19 percent are Roman Catholics.

Bahamian churches range from ornate cathedrals in well-to-do areas to small, one-room buildings scattered throughout the poorer residential neighborhoods. On the Family Islands, every settlement has at least one house of worship. On Sunday mornings, the sound of hymns and spirituals resounds across the islands.

Most Bahamians are Christians, and the islands abound with lovely churches.

In small villages, simple wooden churches serve as meeting places for the faithful.

Some Family Islanders combine Christian beliefs with *obeah*, or voodoo, an ancient practice also found in Africa and on other Caribbean islands. Family Islanders also maintain other traditional practices, such as the old Bahamian tradition of courtship. When a young man turns 18, he usually begins looking for a wife. First, he asks a young woman's family for permission to visit her home. If, after he has courted her, the young man wishes to marry the woman, he presents her with a ring and a letter of his intentions. If the woman's mother decides against the marriage, she simply returns the letter.

After a marriage has been agreed upon, the young man is expected to build and furnish a home for his intended bride. The marriage cannot take place until the house is built. The islands are scattered with homes-in-progress that prospective bridegrooms are building.

Holidays and Festivals

Bahamians observe many public holidays, including New Year's Day, Good Friday, Easter Monday, Whit Monday (the eighth Monday after Easter), Labor Day (the first Friday in June), Independence Day (July 10), Emancipation Day (the first Monday in August), Discovery Day (October 12), Christmas Day, and Boxing Day (December 26). They celebrate some of these holidays with lavish festivals and parades.

On Boxing Day and again on New Year's Day, Bahamians hold a festive parade called Junkanoo. Before dawn, individuals and groups parade through the streets dressed in elaborate costumes, masks, and headdresses made from colorful crepe paper. Moving in a slow, dancing march called rushing, the masked revelers blow whistles and ring cowbells to the beat of goatskin drums.

Revelers dressed in colorful costumes parade through the streets during Junkanoo.

Some people believe that Junkanoo originated during the days of slavery, when the slaves were given time off to celebrate the holidays with African dance, music, and costume. Today, the Junkanoo is an organized event in which six major adult groups and several juvenile groups compete for prizes. In order to be considered for competition, each group must choose a theme about the Bahamas. They are judged on the basis of performance, music, and originality of costumes.

The exact origin of the word Junkanoo is unknown. Some think it comes from the French term *gens inconnus,* which means unknown people (a reference to the masks worn by the participants). Others claim that the celebration is named after John Conuu, or Conny, an 18th-century African prince who demanded the right to celebrate with his people even after being brought to the West Indies as a slave.

In July and August, the Bahamians hold the Goombay Summer Festival, named after the islands' traditional goombay music. Begun in 1971, the festival was designed to expose visitors to all aspects of Bahamian culture—religion, folk music, cuisine, sports, and folklore depicting the country's colorful past.

Tales of Fancy

Myth and folklore abound in the Bahamas, especially on the Family Islands. Many islanders believe in mythical creatures, buried treasure, and fantastic legends. Some believe that the Fountain of Youth is located on the island of Bimini, and others claim that the large, underwater stone formations found on North Bimini are part of the lost city of Atlantis.

Many islanders also believe in the chickarnies—three-toed, red-eyed elves who will turn a person's head around if he does not treat them with respect. According to legend, the chickarnies hang from their toes in trees on the island of Andros. Another mythical creature is the elusive Lusca, who is allegedly half dragon and half octopus. Lusca is said to live in a cave and to devour anyone who comes near him.

On Little Exuma Island, two different legends explain the naming of Pretty Molly Bay. In the first, Molly is said to have been a pretty young slave who drowned herself in the bay and now roams the beach at night. The other version claims that Molly was a young white woman who was transformed into a mermaid and now sits on a rock in the bay, combing her hair by moonlight.

A popular Inagua Island legend involves Henri Christophe, the Haitian revolutionary leader who crowned himself king in 1811. Although historians believe that Christophe committed suicide in 1820, many islanders claim that he escaped to Inagua and hid in its dense forests. In 1920, American playwright Eugene O'Neill used this legend as the basis for his play *The Emperor Jones*.

The Bahamas's pirate history has created tales of buried treasure on almost every island. Some of these treasure legends are myths, but others have been proved true. Treasure has been found on Cat Island and in shipwrecks in the coral reefs. In 1986, treasure-hunters located the wreck of the Spanish galleon *Nuestra Señora de la Maravilla* ("Our Lady of Wonder") about 50 miles (80 kilometers) north of Grand Bahama Island. Treasure retrieved from the ship, which sank in 1656, is worth many millions of dollars.

The Arts

Singing, dancing, painting, and writing are integral parts of Bahamian culture. Traditionally, most of the islands' art was created for pleasure rather than profit. But the growth of an arts industry has altered this somewhat, allowing some Bahamians to profit from their talents. And Bahamians themselves have begun to respect island arts. Each year, the Bahamas holds the National Arts Festival to recognize local achievements in drama, dance, painting, sculpture, and music.

(continued on page 73)

here come.the BRIDE
PAINT BY MR AMOS
FERGUSON
1984

SCENES OF
BAHAMAS

➤ *Picturesque coastal towns dot the Family Islands, where life is slow and simple.*

▲ *Junkanoo participants are judged on the originality of their colorful costumes.*

◄ *Children receive excellent educations at schools that follow British techniques.*

◄ *Bahamian craftspeople practice ancient arts, such as building boats by hand.*

⋎ *Bays and lagoons typify the Bahamas's coastline.*

ʌ *The Abaco Lighthouse helped ships navigate the treacherous Bahamian coasts.*

➤ *The hauls of fishermen like these provide a large portion of the Bahamian diet.*

▲ *Historic castles recall the Bahamas's years as a battleground.*

◄ *Exotic flamingos thrive in the warm Bahamian climate.*

◄ Above-ground crypts
surround a church in
George Town.

➤ Sculptured gardens,
such as this one in
Nassau, attract
thousands of visitors.

◄ Unusual tropical flowers
flourish in Bahamian
gardens.

◄ *The value of colorful Bahamian currency is tied to the worth of the U.S. dollar.*

➤ *Glamorous hotels, including the Royal Bahamian, attract tourists to the islands.*

(continued from page 64)

Until recently, most Bahamians did not recognize the value of their folk art. They took for granted their traditional crafts, such as conch-shell jewelry, carved wooden figures, and brightly painted Androsia cloth from the Family Islands. But in 1983, Bahamian painter Amos Ferguson became famous for his colorful, two-dimensional works featuring island and religious themes. A collection of his works appeared in museums in the United States, and he received acclaim for his artistry.

Other artists who are well-known in the Bahamas include Dennis Knight, an Englishman who fashions pottery; Ivy Simms, a Long Island native who makes straw work to sell in Nassau's Straw Market; and Stephen Burrows, an untrained sculptor. Burrows uses scrap metal to produce his larger-than-life sculptures, which can be seen throughout Nassau's parks and public areas.

The Bahamas has a long tradition of performance arts. Bahamian dance has been influenced by many other cultures. Older Bahamians enjoy the quadrille, a type of square dance that originated in Europe. In the Bahamas, this structured dance takes on an African flavor. Other Bahamians favor the jump dance, in which one person at a time dances inside a circle to a five-beat drum accompaniment. One of the best-known dances in the Bahamas is the limbo, a West Indian dance in which flexible dancers bend backward and shimmy under a low pole. In 1976, the National School of Dance was founded to preserve these dances.

Most Bahamian folk music is centered around the Junkanoo beat, which relies on resonance from a goatskin drum. In the past, the islanders used wooden barrels to make all of their drums, but they now make most of them from tin oil drums. Junkanoo is often intertwined with calypso, another heavily percussive style of music developed in the Caribbean.

Not all Bahamian music is folk music. The Royal Bahamas Police Force Band serves as the national concert band, performing at

A craftsperson displays woven purses, hats, and other wares at Freeport's Strawmarket.

national ceremonies. The New Providence Consulate Band, a collection of high-school musicians, also plays on important occasions. It was organized to perform for Britain's Queen Elizabeth when she visited the Bahamas in 1977. Children are required to take music as a standard school subject until the ninth grade. They are encouraged to play in the school orchestra, sing in the choir, and seek private musical instruction.

The Bahamas's literary tradition is largely an oral one. In the 20th century, however, many Bahamian folk tales have been preserved in writing. *Cocoa Plumming,* by Mizpah Tertullien, records an adventure of Br'er Rabbie and Br'er Bookie, favorite Bahamian folk characters. These characters appear in stories in many West Indian islands. In the southern United States, these tales appear as the Br'er Rabbit stories.

Some Bahamian authors and poets write in formal English, but most write in the local dialect, which has the most authentic sound. Their plots often teach a moral lesson. Susan J. Wallace, a well-known Bahamian poet and playwright, captures the essence of Bahamian life in her poem "Islan' Life," written in dialect. The final stanza emphasizes the importance of community to the Bahamian:

Islan' life ain' no fun less ya treat errybody
like ya brudder, ya sister, or ya frien'
Love ya neighbour, play ya part, jes' remember das de art,
For when ocean fenc' ya in, all is kin.

The Bahamas's major theater, the Dundas Center for the Performing Arts, produces both Bahamian and foreign plays. Bahamian playwright Winston Saunders, author of the critically acclaimed *You Can Bring a Horse to Water*, has served as the theater's director. Amateur

The Royal Bahamas Police Force Band plays concert music at many ceremonial occasions.

theaters on the islands include the Freeport Players' Guild and the Grand Bahamas Players.

How the Bahamians Relax

Sport is an important thread in the Bahamian social fabric. In 1977, the Bahamian government organized the Ministry of Youth, Sports, and Community Affairs to coordinate the islands' sporting interests. Bahamians participate in basketball, volleyball, track and field, and a variety of other events.

The favorite sport in the Bahamas is softball. Bahamian softball teams compete in the World Softball Conference and frequently outdo competitors from their Caribbean and Central American neighbors. Other popular sports include basketball and volleyball, which many Bahamian students play in intramural and interscholastic competition. Playing basketball and volleyball has helped many Bahamians win scholarships to colleges and universities in the

Volleyball, a popular sport in the Bahamas, has earned many students American scholarships.

*Scores of islanders
participate in sailing
events such as the
Family Islands regatta.*

United States. For example, Osborne Lockhart, a Bahamian who won
a basketball scholarship to the University of Minnesota, later played
with the Harlem Globetrotters.

The Bahamians also compete in track and field events. Local
stars participate in regional competitions, such as the Central American and Caribbean Games, and in international competitions, such
as the Olympic, Pan American, and Commonwealth games. Disabled
Bahamian athletes have also won medals in international competitions.

Bahamians and visitors alike enjoy a variety of water sports.
Serious fishermen can participate in the many year-round Bahamian
tournaments that continue to produce record-breaking catches. The
islands also host international sailing, windsurfing, and powerboat
events and are famous for local regattas, especially the Family Islands
regatta, held every April in George Town, Exuma.

In addition to the sun and sand, attractions such as landscaped gardens (including the Garden of the Groves, above) bring tourists to the Bahamas.

Touring the Bahamas

Because tourism is such a vital part of the Bahamian economy, the government has taken steps to preserve many of the Bahamas's historic sites and cultural artifacts as tourist attractions. It has also built a variety of parks, gardens, shopping centers, and other recreation areas to lure visitors.

Nassau, the nation's capital, contains the greatest variety of attractions. It is the historic, economic, and cultural heart of the Bahamas. Bay Street, the city's hub, is lined with restaurants, shops, and government buildings. Its focal point is Rawson Square, where the House of Assembly and Supreme Court are located. Near Rawson Square sits Prince George Dock, the city's busiest pier.

Many historic forts, built in earlier times to protect New Providence Island from attack, line Nassau's shores. Fort Montagu was built in 1741 to guard the eastern entrance to Nassau Harbor. Fort Charlotte, the largest fort, has many dungeons and underground chambers. Built during Lord Dunmore's governorship in the late 1700s, it never saw battle. Another fort built during Dunmore's governorship, Fort Fincastle, is noted for the Queen's Staircase. A flight of 66 steps cut into a nearby limestone canyon, the staircase was built by slaves to serve as an escape route for the fort's troops.

Vendors sell their wares by the Queen's Staircase in Fort Fincastle.

Nassau has several beautiful gardens. The Nassau Botanical Gardens, located behind Fort Charlotte, feature paths leading from a cactus garden to a stone grotto that holds a tropical flower garden. Another lush garden is found behind the Royal Victoria Hotel, which was built during the American Civil War and was closed in 1971. Its gardens contain about 300 varieties of tropical plants.

Marine life abounds in and around the Bahamas, including giant sea turtles, sharks, manta rays, and the hundreds of creatures that inhabit the coral reefs. Scuba diving and fishing are major tourist attractions in the Bahamas. In addition to several aquariums on New Providence and Grand Bahama islands, tourists can watch dolphins perform or can swim with them on boat cruises organized by such groups as The Dolphin Experience, operating out of Freeport, and Dolphin Encounters, leaving from Nassau.

Trained dolphins perform for visitors during a show at the Seafloor Aquarium in Nassau.

Paradise Island, which is joined to New Providence by a toll bridge, is a self-contained tourist utopia. In addition to luxurious hotels that provide a full program of sports and recreation for their guests, Paradise Island is the home of the Versailles Gardens. These gardens contain beautiful sculptures, seven formal garden terraces, and a 14th-century French cloister that was brought from France stone by stone and reconstructed.

The Birth of Freeport

Freeport, the Bahamas's other major city, is a major commercial and tourist center. Yet, it did not exist until 1955, when it was

This reconstructed French cloister stands in the Versailles Gardens on Paradise Island.

The Hawksbill Creek Agreement helped developers build hotels.

created as a result of the Hawksbill Creek Agreement. Negotiated by American businessman Wallace Groves, the agreement gave his company, the Grand Bahama Port Authority, exclusive rights to develop 50,000 acres (20,000 hectares) of unused land. Groves and his associates also received special permission to establish the Bahamas's first casino on Grand Bahama Island.

The casino and other development projects, including a harbor, an airport, and educational and medical services, brought thousands of people to Freeport and the neighboring Lucaya resort area. As a result, Freeport has grown into the Bahamas's second largest city. Today, it boasts glamorous hotels, nightclubs, casinos, gourmet restaurants, and recreation facilities.

Tourists and Bahamians alike enjoy Freeport's shopping areas. The International Bazaar, which covers 10 acres (4 hectares) in the heart of Freeport, features exotic wares from 25 different countries. The Chinese and Japanese shops exhibit beautifully embroidered robes and silk-covered jewel boxes. The Middle Eastern shops offer ivory carvings and small, lifelike, wooden animals covered with genuine fur. The African shops sell exotic elephant-hair jewelry. Greek wares, such as hanging shell clusters, are found in the Greek shops.

The 12-acre (4.8 hectare) Garden of the Groves is located near the bazaar in Freeport. Named for developer Wallace Groves and his wife, Georgette, the garden contains a Hibiscus Showcase that features a brilliant display of red, yellow, orange, and pink hibiscus. At the garden's eastern end, a nondenominational limestone chapel, called the Sanctuary, has been built. Near the Sanctuary is the Bougainvillea Walk, which is lined with multicolored rows of the small-flowered bougainvillea shrub.

The Grand Bahama Museum, located at the garden's western end, features many historical exhibits, including a display of Lucayan Indian artifacts and a reconstructed Lucayan burial mound. Nearby, the Fern Gully evokes a feeling of prehistoric times. Boulders, jutting ferns, huge, climbing philodendrons, and fiery-colored croton flowers cover its walls.

National Parks

Several national parks operate in the Bahamas. The Bahamian National Trust, a nonprofit organization that ensures the conservation of the Bahamas's natural heritage, manages many park areas. The Inagua National Park is internationally known as the world's largest breeding colony of West Indian flamingos. Conception Island National Park, located between San Salvador and Long Island, is an important sanctuary for migratory birds.

Lucayan National Park, which covers 40 acres (16 hectares) east of Freeport on Grand Bahama, has the longest underwater cave system in the world, with more than 6 miles (9.6 kilometers) of charted caves. Other parks include the Exuma Cays Land and Sea Park, the Pelican Cays Land and Sea Park, and the Retreat, an 11-acre (4.4-hectare) garden of rare palms located in residential Nassau.

One of the Bahamas's many national parks has been set aside as a flamingo breeding ground.

The Bahamas has a long history, and the Bahamians are proud of their country and traditions. In the 1970s, the Ministry of Tourism introduced the people-to-people program to help tourists get to know Bahamians better. The program introduces tourists to Bahamian families whose leisure, occupational, or religious interests are similar to their own. The tourists spend time with the Bahamians, who take them to local social clubs, churches, or just to see the sights. The government hopes the program will encourage visitors to come back to the Bahamas in the future.

The Bahamas has finally begun to use its natural beauty and warm climate to attract tourists. Thanks to tourism, the economy is now stable.

A Prosperous Nation

For much of its history, the Bahamas faced economic turmoil. Periods of prosperity were frequently followed by hard times. In the latter half of the 20th century, however, the country has diversified its economic base and developed its tourist and financial industries. Today, the Bahamas enjoys a stable economy. It has modern transportation and communications systems and a high standard of living.

Tourism is by far the Bahamas's largest industry. It contributes 60 percent of the country's revenue and employs about one half of all Bahamians. For this reason, the Bahamian government encourages companies to invest their capital in island hotels and resorts. For instance, the Bahamian government passed the Hotels Encouragement Act in 1949. This act, administered by the Ministry of Tourism, encourages developers to build new hotels and refurbish old ones. It refunds all customs duties paid on materials used to construct and furnish the hotel and provides tax breaks once the hotel is in operation.

Tourism is promoted extensively by the Bahamas Ministry of Tourism, the Nassau and Paradise Island Promotion Board, the Grand Bahama Island Promotion Board, the Family Island Promotion Board, and the Bahamas Hotel Association. Their combined efforts have led to steady growth in tourist arrivals, hotel bookings, and tourist expenditures. Since 1950, the number of tourists in the Bahamas has risen from about 45,000 to over 3,500,000 in the late 1990s.

Most of the Bahamas's tourists are Americans, so the government has sought to make financial transactions between Americans and Bahamians easy. It has tied the value of the Bahamian dollar to that of the U.S. dollar, making them equal. This also eases trade between the two countries.

An International Financial Center

The Bahamian government has encouraged the growth of banking and finance, the country's second largest industry, through incentives to its foreign investors. These include freedom from Bahamian taxes and exemption from certain taxes in investors' home countries.

The multimillion-dollar Xanadu resort in Freeport caters to European and American tourists.

Other Bahamian tax laws have also helped attract investors. No income, estate, gift, or inheritance taxes exist. The only direct tax is a real property tax levied on developed properties (and on undeveloped properties, if the owner is a non-Bahamian). The Bahamas also appeals to banks and other investors because of its political stability, judicial independence, and emphasis on the secrecy of relations and transactions between financial institutions.

Since the 1960s, the Bahamas has been a major financial center for offshore investment banking, with over 400 banking and trust companies licensed. Since the International Business Companies Act was passed in 1990, allowing companies to operate anonymously and tax-free, 40,000 other offshore companies have formed. Financial services provide 10 percent of the Bahamas's gross domestic product.

Other Industries

To broaden the Bahamas's economic base, the government encourages the development of other industries. The largest of these is the petroleum industry. Grand Bahama is now the site of two oil refineries, a petroleum transshipment terminal (where oil is transferred from big tankers to smaller ships for individual deliveries), and a petrochemical plant. The government has encouraged further petroleum exploration by allowing foreign companies to search for oil in and around the islands.

The government also encourages the development of agricultural and fishing industries. In the agricultural sector, it works to produce new foodstuffs, expand vegetable and meat production, and construct grain storage facilities. In the fishing industry, the government focuses its efforts on research, training programs, loans to Bahamian fishermen, and the introduction of a fish handling and marketing complex in New Providence.

Other Bahamian industries include drug manufacturing, light equipment assembly, aragonite (a calcium-based mineral) mining,

Oil refining is another recent industry that has helped the Bahamian economy to grow.

and salt production through solar evaporation. In addition, the Bahamas exports fruits, vegetables, fish, and fish products. Also, New Providence is the home of Bacardi and Company, one of the world's largest rum producers.

Encouragement for industrial growth comes in many forms. The Bahamas Development Bank provides financing for new industrial, agricultural, and fishing enterprises and for small businesses, such as craft and clothing manufacturers. The Industrial Encouragement Act of 1970 exempts manufacturers of approved products from customs duty, export taxes, income taxes, and real property taxes under certain conditions. Another piece of legislation, the Caribbean Basin Initiative, grants full duty exemption on manufactured goods exported to the United States.

The Cost of Living

Most items available for sale in the Bahamas—including foodstuffs, clothing, dry goods, hardware, building supplies, motor vehicles, and general merchandise—are expensive because they are imported from the United States, Britain, Canada, or any of the more than 80 countries that export goods to the Bahamas. To ensure that all Bahamians can afford life's essentials, the government controls the prices of many goods under the Price Control Act of 1971. The act regulates the prices of staple foods, such as bread, butter, mayonnaise, rice, sugar, and tomato paste.

The cost of Bahamian housing is about equal to that of housing in the United States. Virtually all homes and apartments available for rent or sale are fully furnished—they even include dishes and cookware. For the tourist, numerous agencies in Nassau and Freeport provide information on accommodations, ranging from hotels and beach houses to apartment rentals.

Although the per capita income of the Bahamas is lower than that of the United States, Bahamians do not pay any income taxes. They are subject only to a modest deduction of about 3.4 percent for national insurance, which is similar to the U.S. social security program. For the most part, Bahamians are prosperous.

Transportation

Like the British who settled the islands, the Bahamians drive on the left side of the road. But unlike the British, they observe speed limits that do not exceed 45 miles (72 kilometers) per hour. The heavily populated islands of New Providence and Grand Bahama have many modern, paved roads. Most of the Family Islands, however, have only one or two roads that extend the length of the island. In these areas, boats are often used instead of cars because most towns can be reached more easily by water.

Few Bahamians own cars. Only about 83,000 motor vehicles are registered in the Bahamas, most of them on New Providence. Those numbers include private vehicles, government-owned vehicles, taxis, rental cars, scooters, and buses. On New Providence and Grand Bahama Island, tourists often use metered taxis whose fares are set by

Bahamians and tourists alike zoom around the islands on convenient motor scooters.

the Ministry of Transport. Rental cars, jitneys (25-seat minibuses), motor scooters, and bicycles are used by Bahamians and tourists.

Boating is the most accessible transportation method in the Bahamas. Large cruise ships moor at ports by the major cities, and power boats and sailboats dock at marinas scattered throughout the islands.

New Providence's main seaport is located at Potter's Cay in Nassau. Grand Bahama has several major ports, including those at Freeport and West End. Most of the Family Islands have many small docks and only one main port, where mail boats dock. For example, in the Abaco islands the mail boat docks at Marsh Harbour, but ferry services operate among the ports of Marsh Harbour, Treasure Cay in the northwest, and, offshore, Elbow and Man-O-War cays.

Many people use mail boats as an inexpensive way to see the Family Islands. Each week, about 20 mail boats leave Nassau. Each boat stops at one or two islands during a trip that takes almost a day and is usually made overnight. The boats carry mail and provisions, and the decks are crowded with freight, produce, livestock, and local commuters. Some passengers share food and shelter with the crew or take along their own food, drinks, and blankets. A few boats provide sleeping quarters and food services.

Most visitors arrive in the Bahamas by airplane. Many foreign airlines fly there every day. Most flights land at either Nassau International Airport on New Providence or the Freeport International Airport on Grand Bahama. However, some small airlines fly from Florida to Abaco, Exuma, Eleuthera, and Bimini. The Bahamian national airline, Bahamasair, flies passengers from several cities in the United States. In addition to the international airports on the major islands, some 50 smaller airfields serve the Family Islands.

Communications

The Bahamas Telecommunications Corporation, a public utility, operates the Bahamas's telephone system and licenses all private radio-telephone stations, including those on marine vessels. Nassau, Freeport, and Eight Mile Rock (on Grand Bahama) have 24-hour telephone and telegraph service to everywhere in the world.

The Bahamas's telephone system provides direct-dial service to and from over 100 countries. In those areas on the Family Islands without local service, mobile telephones are available in cars, boats, and homes. However, the government is moving rapidly to extend full communications throughout the country. A digital satellite communications system connects Switzerland and the Bahamas for the transfer of financial data between two of the world's great banking and financial centers.

The Bahamas has a free press: the government has no control over what is printed. Two country-wide daily newspapers originate in Nassau, the morning *Nassau Guardian* and the afternoon *Tribune*. A local daily, the *Freeport News*, is published on Grand Bahama. Major newspapers from the United States are available on their day of publication; British newspapers arrive a day or two late.

The government owns and operates the Bahamas Broadcasting Corporation, which runs the country's only television station and the major radio stations. Three FM stations run by private companies have started up recently. The government's four radio stations play at least some calypso music during the day. ZNS 1, called Radio Bahama, plays more "oldies" music and hosts talk shows. ZNS 2, known as Radio New Providence, plays a mixture of soft and hard rock and also hosts talk shows. ZNS 3, Radio Grand Bahama, plays popular music. In addition to these three AM stations, there is ZNS FM.

ZNS TV-13, the only television station that originates in the Bahamas, transmits from New Providence and broadcasts to a distance of 130 miles (208 kilometers) from Nassau. It operates during daylight hours on the weekdays, with increased hours of programming on Saturday and Sunday. The staff of the Bahamas Broadcasting Corporation chooses the programming, which includes British and Canadian educational programs, American situation comedies, championship sports,

Satellite dishes allow Bahamians to view television broadcasts from around the world.

and many British Broadcasting Corporation shows. Bahamian news is shown nightly, and religions programs air on Sundays.

In addition, a cable TV system and satellite dishes bring mostly American, Canadian, and British radio and television programs to all parts of the islands. Broadcasts originating in Florida, especially Miami, also reach the Bahamas.

Electricity and Water

New Providence and most of the Family Islands are served by a publicly owned utility, the Bahamas Electricity Corporation. However, Grand Bahama is supplied by a privately owned company, Freeport Power and Light, and some of the Family Islands also use private systems.

The water and sewage systems for New Providence and some of the Family Islands are provided by a government-owned corporation, while, again, Grand Bahama and other Family Islands are supplied by private companies. Water treatment in the Bahamas makes use of the most modern purification methods.

The government has pressed ahead with ambitious plans to bring completely modern water and electric service to the most remote areas of the Family Islands, both to serve the public and to attempt to halt the flow of the population from the Family Islands to Nassau and Freeport.

Hubert Ingraham and the Free National movement (FNM) party came to power in 1992, defeating Lynden Pindling and the Progressive Liberal party (PLP).

The Bahamas Marches On

The Bahamas's history is a history of battles. In the 15th century, the Spanish arrived, beginning more than 300 years of battles for control of the island chain. In 1647, British settlers arrived in the Bahamas. Their settlement was destroyed a half-century later when Spain raided the islands. The British regained control, only to have Spain attack again in 1720. In 1776, as Britain battled for control of its rebellious North American colonies, the United States Navy captured Fort Montagu in Nassau Harbor and held it for several days. In the late 18th century, the islands changed hands repeatedly as Britain and Spain fought for control.

When the British finally won the islands in 1783, the real battle for the Bahamas began. During the next century, the islands faced an economy weakened by the end of slavery and the erosion of the islands' soil. In 1851, they faced another attack, from a cholera epidemic that killed thousands of islanders. In the 20th century, the Bahamas underwent a Quiet Revolution, in which the black majority demanded its civil rights and an end to colonial rule.

In 1973, the Bahamas gained freedom from Britain. The independent Bahamians still face many battles, but today, they are winning them. They have won the battle to revitalize their economy by encouraging tourism and financial investment. They have diversified their economic bases by developing a petroleum industry and a strong shipping enterprise. They have educated themselves, stabilized their government, and modernized their transportation and communications systems. At the same time, the Bahamians have preserved their unique cultural heritage.

After three centuries of struggle, the Bahamas now enjoys political stability and prosperity. It has become a vital member of the world community, with memberships in the United Nations, the Commonwealth of Nations, and a variety of Caribbean organizations.

In early 1973, as the Bahamas prepared for the signing of its independence treaty, the Bahamians redesigned their flag and chose a national anthem. The flag features a black triangle against three horizontal stripes of aquamarine and gold. According to Bahamian officials, black represents the vigor and power of a united people, the triangle represents the Bahamas's determination to develop its resources, and the stripes represent those resources—the land and the sea, symbolized by gold and aquamarine.

The Bahamian national anthem is called "March on Bahamaland." Its lyrics capture the spirit of the Bahamian people:

> Lift up your head to the rising sun, Bahamaland;
> March on to glory, your bright banner waving high.
> See how the world marks the manner of your bearing!
> Pledge to excel thro' love and unity.
> Pressing onward, march together to a common loftier goal;
> Steady sunward, tho' the weather hide the wide and treach'rous
>   shoal.
> Lift up your head to the rising sun, Bahamaland;
> 'Til the road you've trod leads unto your God,
> March on, Bahamaland!

◄GLOSSARY►

Ambergris	A waxy substance found in tropical waters that is used in making perfume.
Androsia cloth	Brightly printed cloth made in the Family Islands.
Archipelago	A chain of islands that are part of the same undersea mountain formation.
Atoll	A low-lying island, found in tropical or subtropical latitudes, consisting of a coral reef surrounding a lagoon.
Bajamar	Spanish for "low water." A reference to the Bahamas's shallow waters and the source of the country's name.
Barrier reef	A long coral reef separated from land by a wide lagoon.
Blue hole	A column of fresh water in the ocean that rises from a buried cave, sometimes far from the nearest land.
Boiling hole	An underground passage that allows fresh water to flow into the sea or seawater to flow inland at certain tides.
Cay	A low-lying island or reef made of coral or sandstone.
Conch	A shellfish that is a staple food in the Bahamas.
Coral reef	A ridge of layered limestone that forms when tiny sea creatures called polyps shed their skeletons.

Fringe reef A tall coral structure at the edge of the shallow water surrounding an island.

Jump dance An island dance performed by a dancer in the center of a circle to a five-beat drum accompaniment.

Junkanoo A festival and parade held on Boxing Day and New Year's Day.

Mulatto A person of mixed black and white ancestry.

Obeah A voodoo practice found in varying degrees throughout the Caribbean area. Obeah has its origin in traditional African religions, but it is greatly influenced by Christianity in some communities.

Quadrille A European square dance whose Bahamian form is strongly influenced by African dance and music.

◄ INDEX ►

ACKNOWLEDGMENTS

The author and publishers are grateful to the following sources for photographs: AP/Wide World (p. 96); Architect of the Capitol (p. 28); Associated Press (pp. 24, 26, 39, 40, 52); Bahamas News Bureau (pp. 2, 14, 16, 18, 23, 48, 56, 58, 59, 60, 61, 62, 66, 67, 68a, 68b, 69a, 69b, 70b, 70c, 71a, 71b, 72a, 72b, 74, 75, 77, 81, 82, 83, 85, 86, 88, 90, 92); Bahamian Tourist Office (pp. 20, 70a, 78, 80); Bettmann Archive (p. 38); Central Office of Information, London (p. 45); Department of the Archives, Nassau, Bahamas (pp. 44, 55); Library of Congress (pp. 34, 37); National Maritime Museum, Greenwich (pp. 32, 33); New York Public Library Picture Collection (p. 35); PAR/NYC (pp. 30, 76); Third Wave Communications (p. 94); Wadsworth Atheneum (p. 65); Wide World (pp. 42, 46, 51, 53). Picture Research: PAR/NYC.